Tryouts

I reached to pick up the ball we had thrown just a moment before. My bare brown hand squeezed the seams as hard as I could, and I felt the rough black thread bite my fingers. The smooth white horsehair cover was unyielding, but I kept on squeezing it to keep from crying.

I rotated the ball around and around in my palm until it felt strong and familiar again. And then I knew I had to throw it at least once.

And so I drew myself in tight, cocked my front leg, reared back as far as I could go, and whipped my arm forward to throw. The black-and-white ball singed the air hard and fast across the open field. It landed right where I wanted it to—in the dirt just beyond home plate.

A yellow-haired player in uniform shaded her eyes toward me, then bent down to pick it up. She stood there, they all stood there, whispering and looking right at me, no one daring to throw it back. The men saw it too. We were good, and we knew we were good. And now they knew it too.

✧ ✧ ✧

"The reader is richer for the opportunity of meeting Mamie in this poignant and fascinating story of a great lady."

—*Kirkus Reviews*

"Peppered with colorful language and filled with Johnson's natural exuberance and love of life . . . this is an enjoyable account of a part of history that will come as a surprise to many readers."

—*BCCB*

OTHER BOOKS YOU MAY ENJOY

Between Madison and Palmetto	Jacqueline Woodson
Choosing Up Sides	John H. Ritter
Last Summer With Maizon	Jacqueline Woodson
Maizon at Blue Hill	Jacqueline Woodson
Mayfield Crossing	Vaunda Micheaux Nelson
Over the Wall	John H. Ritter
Rosa Parks: My Story	Rosa Parks
Strike Two	Amy Goldman Koss
A Whole New Ball Game	Sue Macy

A STRONG RIGHT ARM

The Story of Mamie "Peanut" Johnson

MICHELLE Y. GREEN
Introduction by Mamie Johnson

PUFFIN BOOKS

PUFFIN BOOKS
Published by Penguin Group
Penguin Young Readers Group,
345 Hudson Street, New York, New York 10014, U.S.A.
Penguin Books Ltd, 80 Strand, London WC2R ORL, England
Penguin Books Australia Ltd, 250 Camberwell Road, Camberwell, Victoria 3124, Australia
Penguin Books Canada Ltd, 10 Alcorn Avenue, Toronto, Ontario, Canada M4V 3B2
Penguin Books (N.Z.) Ltd, 182-190 Wairau Road, Auckland 10, New Zealand

First published in the United States of America by Dial Books for Young Readers,
a division of Penguin Putnam Inc., 2002
Published by Puffin Books, a division of Penguin Young Readers Group, 2004

17 19 20 18 16

THE LIBRARY OF CONGRESS HAS CATALOGED THE DIAL EDITION AS FOLLOWS:
Green, Michelle Y.
A strong right arm : the story of Mamie "Peanut" Johnson / by Michelle Y. Green ;
introduction by Mamie Johnson.
p. cm.
Includes bibliographical references.
ISBN: 0-8037-2661-9 (hc)
1. Johnson, Mamie—Juvenile literature. 2. Baseball players—United States—Biography—Juvenile literature.
3. African American baseball players—Biography—Juvenile literature.
4. Women baseball players—United States—Biography—Juvenile literature.
[1. Johnson, Mamie. 2. Baseball players. 3. Women—Biography.
4. African Americans—Biography.] I. Title.
GV865.J5985 G74 2002 796.357'092—dc21 2001028616

Puffin Books ISBN 0-14-240072-6

Printed in the United States of America

To Mamie
and all heroes,
sung and unsung

✧ ✧ ✧

Table of Contents

Introduction *xi*

The Wall *3*

Carolina Summers *5*

Blackberry Sky *11*

Knuckleball *15*

Long Branch *22*

The Tryout *37*

Bannecker Field *47*

Change-up *61*

Full Count *69*

Call Me Peanut *82*

Miller's Field *99*

Appendices

For More *107*

The They Played Baseball Foundation *110*

Acknowledgments

The still, small voice said, "If I write it, they will come."
So I did, and they did. Thank you to each one who came
alongside me to bring this book home.

Thanks to Nikki Grimes for the sharp stick in the back,
the hard chair on my rump, and for believing in me.
To Elizabeth Harding, who, with two words—"Mamie
rocks!"—spurred me on. And to my skillful editor and
mensch, Toby Sherry, for loving the game, and my writing
almost as much.

Thank you, Mom, Dad, Adrienne, and Ollie—baseball
strategist—for pickups, drop-offs, and sleep-overs. And to
my precious sons, Bryan and Evan, whose creativity pro-
vokes me to envy.

To the mighty, mighty Tigers of Upper Marlboro and
the trusty coaching staff of the Upper Marlboro Boys and

Girls Club, who taught me to pitch and play, especially head coach Ray Schliep, assistant coach Dennis Williams, base coach Russell Butler, and dedicated dad Tony Coleman.

To baseball historian and author Bruce Adelson, for laying the groundwork with solid research; Dennis Bose Biddle, president and CEO of the Yesterday's Negro League Players Foundation; Raymond Doswell, curator of the Negro Leagues Baseball Museum; and Gail R. Redman, library director of The Historical Society of Washington, D.C., for their invaluable help. And to Bill Holmes, native Washingtonian, whose genuine love for the city helped fill in all the gaps.

Finally, to my writing angels and cheerleaders: Deborah Danielle, Chuck Duquette, Bryan Green, Anita Merina, Susie Partridge Robinson, and Katherine Silkin. Yea, team!

Introduction
by Mamie "Peanut" Johnson

Honey, I tell you, I don't know what made that young lady come in the store that particular day. All I know was there were so many people marching in and out of the Negro Leagues Baseball Shop that week of the grand opening. That's why Brother Gary—he owns the shop—asked me to be there. You see, the store isn't just for selling books and videos and shirts and things about baseball. It's about educating people, particularly the children, about a history—their history. I wasn't even working there at the time, but I was glad to come out that day to meet folks and answer questions about what it was like in the old days of Black baseball.

I remember I was sitting in the back close by the rack of T-shirts, so any time someone stopped to look at the one with my picture on it, I noticed. I still get a kick out of the way they look at the front, a picture of me playing ball, then turn it around to read my stats on the back. Some folks just keep on flipping past it on the rack, but some stop and take the time to read it. So when this lady pulled my shirt down from the rack, that's when she caught my eye. She was too busy doing what she was doing to pay me any mind at all. But after a few minutes she started making her way to the register.

I got so tickled at the way she kept asking Brother Gary all these questions about the woman on the shirt. He was trying to help so many folks with so many questions, but she just kept jumping right in there with another question every time she got the chance. Finally I spoke up.

"Would you like me to sign that for you?" That was my way of letting her know that I could answer all her questions about the shirt because the woman on the front was me. Well, honey, she wheeled around, and you shoulda seen the look on her face. That's the other part I like, any time someone finds out that's really me. Most folks don't believe me at first. Some don't believe me at all when I tell them I was one of only three women to ever play professional baseball. But she musta believed me on the spot, because the next thing I know, she made a beeline over to where I was sitting. The first question was: "You're Mamie 'Peanut' Johnson?" And the second question was: "Has anyone written your story?"

Now, nobody'd asked me that question before, sugar, but I'd sure been waiting a long time to hear it. I'd been looking for someone to help me get my story down. And when she started making notes on the back of a store flyer, I kinda felt that this young lady with the T-shirt might just be the one.

That young lady is Michelle Y. Green, and for two years or more she's tracked behind me to baseball games, practices, and baseball card shows. She's worn out the carpet in the store, where I work now, and my ear on the

Mamie and Michelle Green holding up the shirt that brought them together.

phone. So when people ask me who is this nosy "so and so" who keeps asking me all these questions, I just wink at her and say, "That's my daughter."

Michelle says I'm a living legend. I like to say I'm living proof that dreams can come true. You can make up your own mind when you read my story. But I know one thing that she and I agree on—it's important to have a dream and to see it on through.

Do you have a dream? If you don't, maybe my story will get you started working on one. If you do, darling, you're already halfway to making it come true.

A STRONG
RIGHT ARM

The Wall

Mama never mentioned it, but I'm sure I musta been born with a baseball in my hand, its smooth white skin curving into my tiny brown palm. Ever since I can remember, my thoughts flooding back over sixty years now, my life has been wrapped up in that three-inch universe of twine and leather. It's always been that way with me, and I expect it always will be.

Another reporter called me today. Wants to know how I felt about them tearing down County Stadium in Milwaukee to make way for a new one. My name is on a wall there—me, Mamie "Peanut" Johnson—on the Negro Leagues Wall of Fame. Right up there with Ted "Double Duty" Radcliffe,

Josh Johnson, Verdell "Lefty" Mathias, and some of the other fellas, the greatest names in baseball you never knew.

I told him I didn't mind the tearing down as long as what they built is something better. In some ways, that's what my life has been about: tearing down walls to build something better. But I didn't use a bulldozer or a crane. Not a jackhammer or a single stick of dynamite. I used that little three-inch ball, a strong right arm, and a dream of playing baseball. And for more than sixty years now, that's been enough.

Carolina Summers

Summers in South Carolina, where I lived with my grandma Cendonia Belton, were always hot, but not city hot. In Ridgeway, South Carolina, in 1945, the heat had room to move around, to swirl up the dust and bother the sweet gum trees. It got carried around on the backs of dragonflies and dazzled the clothesline tea towels into brilliant white. It settled on screen doors and stuck to the backs of necks.

Summer was too hot for baseball, Grandma said. Yet every day, soon as we could break away from her watchful eye, Leo and me and the other kids around would be out in the yard to play.

Leo, we called him "Bones," was my uncle, but close enough to me in age to be my big brother. He

Mamie first lived with her grandmother Cendonia Belton, in Ridgeway, South Carolina

marked out the bases every day, like we didn't already know that the pie plate was first, the broken piece of flower pot was second, and the large root about three feet from the lilac bush was third. And when we'd slide into home plate, we'd always be sliding over the smooth white lid of a five-gallon bucket of King Cane sugar, the sweetest in the South.

"Bones," Mamie's uncle Leo Belton, was her first baseball teammate and coach

I was ten, and it was my job to get the ball. For that I didn't have to go to the dry goods store two miles away, or to Thorntree School to beg "No Legs" Levi, our principal, for one. All I had to do was find a nice-size rock and wrap it round and round with sticky tape till it had a good heft. They let me get the ball 'cause I was always the one throwing it. I loved everything about baseball, but it was pitching I loved the best. Oh sure, I could run the bases faster than a jackrabbit, but nothing made me grin on the inside like pitching.

I liked the standing up tall. The looking the other

fella in the eye. The sizing him up for a change-up or fastball. And then the pitch. And I didn't pitch like a girl either. Bones made sure of that. Not an underhanded fling of the ball. But a surefire, windup, coming-right-at-ya pitch smack dab over the plate. One that let him know I meant business. One that could tear the bark right off the tree branch the other fella was using for a bat.

Grandma said the pitcher's mound was no place for a girl. Even my best friend, Mary Alice Quales, who was pretty and who all the boys liked, didn't hold any truck with baseball. But baseball was what I liked. The only thing better was a package from home.

Ridgeway was where I lived with Grandma, but my real home was Washington, D.C. Just about every month I'd get a package from my mama, who lived there and worked hard to support me. There would always be a letter promising she'd be down for a visit soon. Or that she'd be sending for me to come live with her without ever mentioning a date. Sometimes there'd be a fancy new dress from Lansburgh's, or a coat if it was wintertime. Never a baseball. But that was okay. I knew Mama loved me and was doing the best she could. My daddy had walked out of Mama's life before I took my first steps. But Grandma had enough love for Mama and me to see us through.

Mamie's mother, Della Belton, circa 1935

Besides, Grandma's house in Ridgeway was big enough to hold all my dreams. It had eighteen rooms and sat on eighty-one acres. It had fruit trees of every kind—plums, peaches, and pears—running streams, and no fences. Maybe I dreamed such big dreams because there was plenty of room to spread them out in Ridgeway. Room for them to run and stretch and grow.

I remember thinking the city was no place for big dreams. They'd get all cramped up and bent. Like trying to throw a fastball with your arm cocked. In my room in Ridgeway, I could look out into the night sky and see starlight. A wide-open sky where my dreams could run. Once I saw a shooting star. God must like baseball, I imagined. He's got a fastball good as mine.

Blackberry Sky

I never saw Bones run so fast. Not when rounding the bases on a pop-up fly ball or busting toward the house for Sunday chicken. Mary Alice and I were halfway down the road to town. She'd been sent to fetch a nickel's worth of lunch meat for supper that day and wanted some walking company. Mary Alice was afraid of snakes, but I didn't mind chancing snakes if it meant we could share the wild blackberries that sprung up beside the road. The store was a good piece away, so we were taking our purple-stained ease as we walked.

I could hear Bones coming before I saw him, the sun-baked stones kicking up from his heels. And I could tell from his scrunched-up face that something was dreadful wrong.

"Mamie . . . come quick," was all he said.

"It's okay," said Mary Alice. "I'll go on ahead."

I took off behind Bones, neither one of us talking. The Carolina sun stung in my throat, and the lump building in my stomach made the running hard.

The big front yard was a commotion of people. I saw Esther Wheeling, a neighbor lady from the church, my great-uncle Caleb and great-aunt Mozell, who lived some two miles away, and Doc Dobson, who mostly came for the fever or to deliver babies. And I knew Grandma wasn't having no baby.

"Bones, what is it?" I finally asked him. "Where's Grandma?"

"Your mama's coming in tomorrow," Bones said. "That's what they told me." He stood a distance from the front porch.

"Well, come on then," I said, but he just stood there silent. Like a big old shade tree with his feet planted, his hands deep down in his pockets, looking toward the house.

I made a move toward the house, but just then

Rev. Adams appeared in the doorway. He made his way through the crowd, turned me around by the shoulders, and told me to wait.

"Where's Grandma?" I begged. Now, I don't give up tears easy, but that lump in my stomach seemed to have moved up into my chest, through my lungs, and into my eyes to squeeze them out. Without answering, he walked me over to where Bones was still standing.

"Children," he said, "your grandma . . . Mrs. Belton, she's with the Lord now. She's at peace."

"How?" Bones spoke into the dust.

"A stroke. It came quick and took her away this morning early." Rev. Adams folded his long body and squatted down to look at me eye level.

"Don't you worry about a thing, honey. Your mama will be here tomorrow, and everything will be all right."

That night Bones and I stayed at Aunt Mozell and Uncle Caleb's place while they got Grandma ready for the viewing. Mama was coming in on the early bus from Washington and would be there by the time I woke up. But I couldn't sleep at all. Grandma taught me about counting stars whenever

I couldn't sleep. It didn't help. They were the same stars I saw night after night from my room at Grandma's, but some of them seemed missing.

What happens now? Who will take care of me? Where will I live? The questions kept coming until the blackberry sky turned to grayish dawn, then pink and red into full day.

"Mamie," called Aunt Mozell from the front room. "Get up, honey, your mama's here."

Knuckleball

"Hi, sugar. How's my baby?" Mama folded me into her pretty brown arms. It had been too long since our last hug, but Mama and I always fit back together just right.

After a long time with me not talking, I looked up. I wanted to memorize her wonderful face. She didn't look too much different from the last time, but I could tell she was tired from the long bus ride. And she'd been crying too, 'cause her eyes were red, and puffy as flour dumplings. Grandma was her mama, and now there was nobody to hold her just like this. I buried my face into her flowery dress again and held on extra tight.

"I'm fine, Mama," I finally said, trying to make

her feel better. "Grandma must be pretty fine too, walking around big old heaven with Granddaddy."

"Bless your heart, child," Mama said, smiling a little. "She's probably telling him what a fine young lady you're turning out to be."

What happened the rest of that day was all a blur. Mama didn't let me and Bones see Grandma right away, not till the people from Chester's Funeral Home got finished. When I did see her, she was laid out all pretty, like she was just sleeping on a soft white cloud. Lots and lots of people came past to pay their last respects. And lots of pies and plates of chicken came too. The grown-ups kept trying to feed me the whole time, like missing Grandma would be easier on a full stomach. But I didn't eat too much.

It was days before Mama sat me down to answer the million and one questions on my mind.

"Let's take a walk," she said suddenly as the sun was fixing to go down. The fireflies were just starting to do their twinkly dance in the air.

We walked around a bit talking about nothing in particular, then she brought me back round by the creek below the house. Grandma had called it her thinking place, and I had seen her sit out there plenty of times. Mama and I sat together on the mossy bank and watched the clear water splashing about the rocks in front of us.

"You know I'm gonna have to be leaving pretty soon," Mama said real plain, "to go back to work." It was hard to see her face clearly in the darkening night, but her voice was all trembly. I tossed a stone into the cool, clear water and watched it trouble the surface. "Aunt Mozell and Uncle Caleb will look after your grandma's things until I can send for them."

"Will you send for me too?" I asked. I could feel myself shaking a little, but not from the chill. Mama knotted her warm hands around mine.

"Now, you know how much I'd like to take you with me, but I just can't." Her voice broke. "Not just yet. Not till I got things ready for you. But soon."

"But Mama . . ." I said, snatching my hands back from hers and brushing the wetness from my cheeks.

"Till then you're gonna be moving to Long Branch with your aunt Dorothy and uncle Ed. You met them once when you were real small. You probably don't remember."

I dug my fingernails into my palms to stop from crying. And that's when I noticed Mama was crying too.

"Is it far from here?" I asked, trying to act braver than I felt.

"You'll ride with me on the bus back to Washington and then go the rest of the way with your uncle. They have a nice little house in Long Branch, New Jersey. You'll be closer to me than when you were at Grandma's. Close enough for me to even visit some weekends."

"But what about Bones?" I asked.

"This place belongs to Bones now," Mama said, finally looking up. "He's gonna be the one to take care of it with a lot of help from Mozell and Caleb. But this will always be your home too, and mine."

The whole time it felt like somebody was squeezing my heart real hard like the way you grip a fastball just before you throw it.

"How long before we leave?" I asked.

"Two days from now. Thursday. I'll help you get your things together."

Packing up my things wasn't the hard part. It was the things I couldn't pack that hurt the most. Bones,

Mary Alice, and the others. Even that rusty old pie plate and King Cane sugar lid belonged here.

Everything I knew about baseball I learned from Bones. Who's gonna help me with my change-up and slider now? Do they even *have* baseball in New Jersey? Will there be stars outside my bedroom window?

"C'mon," said Bones on Thursday right before it was time to leave for the bus station. "There's something I wanna show you." I followed him out to the clod of hard dirt that had been my pitcher's mound.

"This is how you throw a knuckleball," he said. In his hand was a scuffed-up baseball. He cupped it firmly like always, but with his fingers more bent.

"Where'd you get that beat-up old ball?" I asked, surprised he could keep something so wonderful a secret till now.

"It might look beat up to you, but this ball's still got a lot of magic in it."

"Magic? What do you mean magic?"

"Grandpa took me to Columbia once to an exhibition game," Bones explained. "To see the Atlanta Black Crackers against the Birmingham Black Barons."

"Who?" I asked. "I never heard of them before."

"Course not," said Bones, faking a pitch. "Me neither, till I saw them with my own eyes." He stopped throwing and looked at me. "Mamie, they looked just like us."

"You mean kids?" I said, confused.

"No, I mean colored. Every single one. Colored baseball players with uniforms and real bats and baseballs just like this. And they were good too."

"How come I've never heard of them, then, and how come their games aren't on the radio?"

"I don't know about all that," he said, winding up, but never throwing the ball. "But I swore I was gonna get good enough to join them one day." He stopped and looked beyond the walnut grove and into the fields beyond. "Guess I won't have much time for baseball . . . too much work."

"But Bones . . ." I said, that stinging coming up in my throat again.

"Now the thing about a knuckleball," Bones kept on, "is that when you throw it, it just seems to float. You never know which direction it's gonna go, not even the one throwin' it." He threw again without releasing the ball. "Now you try it."

Bones put the tattered baseball in my hand and

wrapped my fingers around it with my knuckles popped up. I loved the pinch of real seams beneath my fingertips as I squeezed the gray-white leather tight. He walked behind home plate and squatted down low. I pitched and he caught until Mama called that it was time to go. My last pitch to Bones was a perfect no-hit knuckleball. Slow-motion like, it bumped along in the breeze awhile, then blew itself straight over the plate.

"You'll be needing this in Long Branch," he said, handing me back the ball. "Show those Jersey boys that we country folk know a thing or two about baseball."

Before the stars could wink good-bye in Ridgeway, Mama and me were on the bus. Somewhere around Richmond, Virginia, I fell asleep, my head rocking back and forth on Mama's shoulder, Bones's baseball cradled in my lap. I remember thinking, as I dozed off, that old ball must have been whacked around from place to place quite a bit. But just like Bones said, I felt sure it still had some magic in it. And maybe, just maybe, so did I.

Long Branch

Being the new girl at Liberty Elementary wasn't the worst part of moving to Long Branch. Neither was living with my aunt Dorothy and uncle Ed in a city house, even though there wasn't even one peach tree in their front yard, and not a creek to be found on Brook Street. The worst part was no baseball.

Oh, they had baseball, all right, just not for girls. Girls, Aunt Dorothy kept telling me, were supposed to play softball. Softball? I didn't even like the sound of it. When I go to pitch a ball, ain't nothin' soft about it. So while most of the girls on the team were just learning the basics—like remembering to run if they ever did slip up and hit the ball—I had to unlearn everything I loved about playing hardball.

For one thing, the ball was the wrong size—seemed twice as big as the one Bones had given me. It felt like a big old cantaloupe in my hand. And the coach wouldn't let me wind up and pitch the way I liked. Instead, I had to pitch underhand, like I was throwing feed to a bunch of dumb chickens instead of trying to strike somebody out. I stuck with it as long as I could—three whole games before I up and quit.

"We'll get 'em next time, Mamie," the coach told me after we lost three games straight. "You're coming along just fine."

But I didn't quit because of losing. It was just that with a new home, a new school, a whole new everything, baseball was the only familiar thing I had left. And here they wanted me to change that too.

I never had much in the way of friends other than the kids I played ball with. I wasn't interested in dolls or tea parties and such like the other girls. And not playing baseball, I had no use for boys either. So once I quit the team, I was pretty much left on my own. Uncle Ed kept right on playing catch with me, though, right out front on Brook Street, when he wasn't working to fix up other people's houses or driving the grocery truck for Safeway.

A STRONG RIGHT ARM

Mamie as a girl of twelve, living in Long Branch, New Jersey

"Ease it on in there, Mamie," he'd say, grinning large and smacking his glove with his fist. That's all I needed to fire one in there harder than ever. Uncle Ed even bought me my own glove and taught me how to break it in proper. But it just wasn't the same as playing on a team. Then came the day that changed all that.

I took a shortcut home from school one day and passed a playground I'd never seen before. There on the dirt field was a whole group of white boys just pitching and hitting and fielding, and having such a good time. Liberty Elementary, where I went to school, was for coloreds only, so I wasn't exactly used to seeing a whole lot of white folks, period. Now, I was always raised to believe that God didn't make us any different, but I also knew that God must not have gotten around to delivering that same message to everybody. That's why Uncle Ed and Aunt Dorothy told me not to socialize with "them." So, I sat my books down, squatted by the fence, and stayed to watch until they finished up.

"You guys look pretty good," I said to a carrot-haired boy, the first to squeeze through the gate past me.

"Whadda you know about it?" he said.

"Give me that ball and I'll show you."

"You're just a dumb old girl, and you're colored besides."

"A ball's a ball all the same," I said. "It don't know nothing about the person who's throwing it except if they're good or not."

"Hey, fellas," he called to his buddies. "Listen up. This colored girl thinks she can play ball."

"I don't think nothing," I hollered louder than him. "I know I can play good as you."

"She even talks funny," said the one with the yellow hair, coming toward me. "Where y'aaaall come from?"

"South Carolina," I said, "where we don't forget our manners."

"South Carolina?" said carrottop. "Well, that's a long way from here."

"This ain't no watermelon-eating contest, you know," said the freckly-faced fat boy with the blue cap on. "This is baseball."

"Yeah," chimed in another. "Didn't your mammy teach you nothing?"

"That's a laugh." The yellow-haired boy snapped a pink bubble right in my face.

Something got stuck in my throat, and I could feel my hands balling up beside me. But before I could do anything, some grown-up interrupted.

"What's the trouble here?" the man asked.

"This colored girl thinks she can play ball. Tell her she can't, Coach."

The tall man dusted off his blue pants and said, "Well, it's a free country." He sized me up and down. "You ever play organized ball?"

"Yes, sir. I played softball for three weeks, then I quit," I said, unballing my fists just a little.

"Softball too tough for you, honey?" he said. The boys laughed together. My face started stinging like I'd eaten too many of Grandma's sweet peaches.

"In case you're interested," he continued, "this club is in the Police Athletic League. We play hardball, and only the best are good enough to play. You live around here?"

"Yes, sir," I answered. "You're a policeman?"

"That's right," said the man in the blue pants. "We sponsor the team."

Now, I wasn't no ugly child, and I'd always been told to respect policemen, so when he told me to run along home, I did just that without another word. But once I got back to the house on Brook

Street, got scolded for not coming straight home from school, and was back in my bedroom, I got to thinking.

I looked out my window at the starless night, and I remembered what Grandma had always told me. Stuff like "The Good Lord helps those who help themselves," and "The truth will set you free." I thought about Bones and Grandma's big old front yard where I used to play. Then I thought about how much fun those boys were having, and me, sitting outside the fence, watching.

The man in the blue pants had said this was a free country, didn't he? That's what we learned in school. Police officers are supposed to uphold the law, and a girl playing baseball wasn't breaking no laws—or was it? I figured there was only one way to find out.

Number 3 Precinct house was not exactly on the way home from school, but my teacher told me it wasn't far.

The redbrick building had four tall columns in front and a huge white door smack dab in the middle. The building took up almost half a city block. I knew right away that was the place, 'cause there were more policemen coming in and out of there than I had seen in my whole entire life. I hitched up my socks, patted down my hair, and marched right on in just like I owned the place.

"Pardon me, sir," I said to the policeman behind the long wooden counter almost taller than me.

"Talking to me, missy?" he said, peering down at me behind round gold glasses. He wore a policeman's uniform that had three important-looking stripes on the shoulder, so I figured he must be the boss.

"Are there any laws in Long Branch about girls playing baseball?"

"Girls playing baseball?"

The way he answered me, I thought maybe he wasn't the boss after all. He wasn't wearing a policeman's hat, which was a shame, 'cause he was balder than a baseball. Then again, I musta looked like no baseball player he'd ever seen. Socks that wouldn't stay up, bangs that wouldn't stay down, and even though it was my best school dress, it was a dress just the same. He looked me up and down awhile.

"Who wants to know?" he said finally.

"Me, sir," I said. "I want to play baseball on that

police team, but I don't want to be breaking no laws." This time, he stood up and came around in front of the counter.

"Police team? You mean the P.A.L. club? You're gonna have to talk to Officer Campbell about that. He's the coach."

"I know, sir. I talked to him yesterday."

"Well, what'd he say?"

"He said it's a free country. So, if it's not breaking any laws, I'd like to know where I sign up."

"Wait a minute, little lady. It's a free country and all, but that don't mean you can just come busting in here and—"

About that time, we heard a commotion coming in the door.

"Sarge, I got one here for booking." It was that policeman from before. Officer Campbell. And he was holding a scruffy-looking guy in handcuffs who smelled like three-day-old catfish. He didn't recognize me at first.

"Excuse me, Officer Campbell, sir," I said. "Is this where I sign up?"

"Well, I'll be. Didn't I just see you yesterday? You in some kinda trouble?"

"I don't want no trouble, sir," I said, "and Mr. Sarge here says I ain't breaking no laws. I just want to play ball. Is this where I sign up?"

By now, everyone around had stopped working. Even the fella in handcuffs was looking at me strange.

"That's the one you should be locking up," he snickered.

"Shut up, Kelly," Officer Campbell said to the smelly man. Then he said to me, "What's your name, girl?"

"Mamie, sir. I live with my aunt and uncle on Brook Street, remember?"

Officer Campbell looked around a bit like he didn't know what to make of it all.

"Look, why don't you just go on and step outside," he told me. "Go on now, I'll be along in a minute."

I guess I shoulda been plenty scared. But Grandma always said if you ain't done nothin' wrong, you ain't got nothin' to be scared of. And so I just sat there on the front steps of that big old building and waited.

When Officer Campbell finally came out, he had a ball, a glove, and a bat with him.

"Okay then, let's see what you got," he said, handing me the bat.

"If it's all the same to you, sir," I said, handing it back to him, "pitchin's what I like."

"That so?" He grinned. "This ain't softball, girlie. We throw 'em like in the big leagues. You ever been to a real game?"

"No, sir," I admitted, "but I can pitch 'em just the same. Fastballs, change-ups"—I hesitated a bit—"and knuckleballs."

Next thing I knew, he was grabbing me by the shoulders, spinning me around, and planting me facing the brick precinct wall about ten feet out.

"Let's see your fastball," he said, squatting with his back to the wall.

When it started getting a little too dark to see, he finally let me stop. My right arm felt like I'd been hauling five-gallon water buckets from Grandma's creek all day, but I didn't dare stop till he told me.

"Tomorrow," he said. "Four o'clock sharp, at that playground you saw us at, you hear? And don't be one minute late. And tell your folks to sign these papers. They know how to read, don't they?"

"Yes, sir," I said. "My aunt's a teacher." I took the papers from Officer Campbell, then I thought to ask, "Excuse me, sir . . . what are you gonna tell the boys?"

He laughed out loud.

"We don't have to tell them one blessed thing, Mamie," he said, calling me by name for the first time. "How 'bout we let that strong right arm of yours do all the talking?"

Well, that arm of mine talked that next day, and it kept on talking loud and clear, right on up to the division championships. We won two years running. Oh, those boys did their share of muttering, but my pitching was good enough to shut them up right quick. Even carrottop stopped squawking when he saw my knuckleball for the first time, just like Bones said.

My aunt and uncle didn't make much of a fuss once they learned what I'd done to get on the team. They let me know that whatever I wanted to do, as long as it wasn't getting in trouble, they were behind me 100 percent. They must not have minded my socializing with white folks after all, seeing how they came out to watch most of my games.

My classmates and teachers didn't make much of it either. In fact, once they got used to the idea, no-body seemed to make a big deal of the fact that I was the only girl and the first colored to play in the Long Branch P.A.L. club. I never thought much of it at the time. In fact it was five years later, when I was fifteen and sitting in Mama's new house in Washington, D.C., that I thought about it at all. In 1947 we were watching TV with the rest of the world as Jackie Robinson, the first colored man to play baseball in the majors, smacked his first hit as a Brooklyn Dodger.

His ball soared into center field and took the hearts and hopes of all colored people with it. Women cheered, and old men cried for joy. Daddies hoisted their brown babies on their shoulders to see it fly, and mothers came out of the kitchen and let supper fix itself. My backbone tingled like the shock of a bat hit hard with a blazing fastball, like the fastball I had first thrown to Officer Campbell a time ago in Long Branch.

The stars over Mama's house in northeast Washington were large as baseballs that night. Or maybe it just seemed that way because Jackie Robinson had opened up a hole in the sky, and the whole world had changed. After decades of being ignored, a colored man was finally in the game, and all America had seen the truth for themselves.

Jackie Robinson, pictured here in his Kansas City Monarchs uniform in 1945, became the first Negro baseball player to cross the color line into the major leagues.
(Courtesy of the Negro Leagues Baseball Museum.)

Jackie was good, and because he was good, other colored ballplayers like Josh Gibson, Satchel Paige, and Roy Campanella might have their shot at the big leagues. They could play with the whole world watching instead of hiding their talents in Negro Leagues teams I had come to know. Teams like the Kansas City Monarchs, the Birmingham Black Barons, and Washington's own Homestead Grays. Proud colored players with strong arms, strong bats, and stronger hearts playing in the dusty fields and peach orchards of sleepy Southern towns.

Too excited to sleep, I thought about baseball and the life ahead of me after high school graduation, just two years away. That night, I slept with Bones's ball under my pillow. Thanks to Jackie Robinson, I was one step closer to the dream.

The Tryout

"C'mon, Rita. I don't plan to be waiting for you all the goll durn day."

"Baseball's waited for a colored woman to play all this time," said Rita. "What makes you think ten more minutes will make a difference?"

Rita Jones was the best first baseman I ever saw. Or maybe I just felt that way 'cause from cradle till now, I had never shared the ballfield with a girl who loved the game as much as me. At seventeen, and fresh out of high school, we played together at St. Cyprian's. It was just a sandlot team, but the word was that scouts sniffed around teams like that all the time. Even Jackie Robinson had swung his bat in the sandlots until somebody important saw the way he could hit.

"We've got to catch the streetcar cross town, then transfer to the bus going into Virginia," I said, thumping the ball over and over in my freshly oiled glove. I was anxious to get going, but mostly I was nervous. And why not? Today could be the day I'd waited for all my life.

"How's your right arm this morning?" Rita said, tying her shoelaces with the speed of a snail in molasses.

"Strong enough to whop you one if you don't come on. We gotta be there by eight, and I want to make sure my arm is warmed up just right. You got enough change for the bus?"

"Sure thing. But I'm hoping we'll only need a one-way fare." Rita stopped tying and looked at me strange-like. "This tryout just might be our ticket into the big time."

She was right. Soon as I'd read the All-American Girls Professional Baseball League was holding tryouts practically in our own backyard, I knew I had to be there. The league had been around about nine years. It started in 1943 during the war, when a lot of fellas traded in their baseball uniforms for a soldier's uniform. Now that World War II was over, and baseball was back in full swing, the All-American Girls weren't as popular as they once were. But they were good. And they got paid. And people still came to see them play. And that was just fine by me. Those gals had busted the door wide open and changed a lot of people's minds about girls and baseball. It was a door I was ready and willing to walk right on through.

I kept thumping the ball.

"Let's not talk about it anymore," I said. "I don't want to jinx nothing." Rita grabbed her gear, and we walked to the corner just in time to catch the streetcar on the first leg of our trip. Before long, we were coming into Virginia.

The back of the bus was crowded for an early Saturday morning. We must have looked a sight, struggling with our balls and bats and gloves to find an open seat. Oh, there were plenty of seats right up front, mind you. But I guess the white people, who had the right to sit in those seats, were sleeping in on this fine Saturday morning. In fact, I only saw six or seven white faces scowl or turn away as we bumped our way into two rear seats close together.

The crowding was all in the back where we coloreds had to sit. Old ladies with stockings sagging down over thick ankles making their way to market. Sleepyhead babies clutching their mamas' apron fronts. Tired-looking men with smeared overalls and sack lunches. And a few who looked like they were going no place in particular. But Rita and me had a place in mind, so it didn't matter much today what we had to go through to get there.

"Where y'all going with those bats?" said a pudgy pink-faced boy across the aisle and a few rows up.

"Leave those coloreds alone," his mama whispered a little too loud, and yanked him around.

"I wanna play ball," whined the boy, still twisting his neck toward Rita and me. "Please, Mama, can't I play too?" Without another word, the boy's mother grabbed him up and moved three rows closer to the front and on the other side. It was like she was saying "If we can't see them, they'll just disappear." But see us or not, we were still there. And the fact was, we wanted to play ball even more than he did. All we needed was a chance.

An hour later, we were crossing a field toward that chance. There must have been a hundred girls clumped around the bleachers. Some of them already wore the skirted uniforms of the All-American

Girls League. Others were there raring at the chance to play the game, eager to make their mark. But even from a distance, it was clear: Not one of them looked like Rita and me.

"Wait," said Rita, pulling me back by my throwing arm. "Let's warm up over here."

"But maybe we're supposed to sign in first," I said, never taking my eyes off of the sweetest field I ever saw.

"Please, Mamie . . ." Rita said. And for the first time I could tell she was afraid. Not just a little nervous like me, but way-down-in-her-socks, choked-in-the-throat scared.

"Rita, what's wrong? Don't back out on me now. All we gotta do is go on out there and play like we always do. Like at St. Cyprian's. Remember that squeaker last week against Anacostia? How we pulled it out at the very end?"

But Rita just stood there, like Bones did that day in the front yard when Grandma died, her long brown arms limp at her side. I wound up and tossed the ball to her gently. Without thinking, she moved her glove to cup the falling ball. It dropped solidly in the pocket and stayed there.

"You go on ahead, Mamie," she said, kicking at a

dirt clod. "Go on and take your shot. It was your idea to come in the first place. I'll just wait here."

"You throw me that ball, Rita. Throw it back to me, you hear. You know we're good enough, and we've come all this way. Let's go show them just how good we are." I pounded my glove over and over with my fist, waiting for her ball to return.

She looped the ball to me, clumsy, like she had never thrown one before. I scooped it up just below my knees and fired it back.

"Ouch," Rita yelped. "What are you trying to do? Break my hand?"

"Better than that no-'count ball you just threw me!"

"Oh, yeah? Well, watch this," she said, her voice a little louder, her throw sure and strong. Again I slammed the ball into her glove. Again. And again. Until she smiled that trouble-coming-at-you smile of hers and gave back as good as she got. For a time, we lost ourselves throwing and fielding the ball: fastballs and change-ups, knucklers and grounders, and high-flying pop-ups. The two of us on a perfect spring morning, with just the ball and the glove, the breeze and the grass, until . . .

"Just what do you two gals think you're doing

here?" the rough man asked as he approached us from the fenced area. He held a clipboard and pen in one hand, an ash-tipped cigar in the other. Rita looked at me, and it was clear they were both waiting for me to answer.

"We're here for the tryouts, sir," I said, standing full up and wiggling my shoulders to straighten them.

"There must be some mistake," he began plainly. "These girls are here to try out for the All-American Girls League," he said, waving his cigar in the direction of the playing field. "You've got the wrong field. Your game must be somewhere else."

"No, sir," I said, fishing in my pocket for the newspaper scrap announcing the tryouts. "We're at the right place."

The man reached for the paper and unfolded it against his clipboard. He glanced at it, then to us, and back again. Then he just stood there for a long time, squinting at us like we were crazy or something. Like we were bothering the grass just by being there.

"I don't think you understand," he said finally, red-faced and firm. He pushed his hat back on his sweat-streaked head. "Just because that colored boy

Robinson and a few of his buddies wormed their way into the majors, doesn't mean we want colored gals playing next to our girls. Now, why don't you two just take off before there's trouble."

By then, everyone on the field had turned our way. Not one of the skirted women who had worked so hard for the right to take to the field, or any of the ones hoping to wear the uniform, took a step in our direction. But two men in striped uniforms started walking toward us at a fast clip, the dust from the infield kicking up beneath their cleated heels.

Rita reached for her bag without a fight.

"C'mon, Mamie. Let's go."

"Wait. Just a minute. We don't want no trouble, sir," I pleaded. "We just want to play ball. Look. I can pitch, and Rita here can field as good as any man."

"That so?" He sneered, tapping his ashes to the ground at our feet. "Well let's see how fast you can run." He waved his cigar in frantic circles. "I'm in charge, and I'm saying that if you don't hightail it out of here right now, I'll have you thrown out." He looked over his shoulder at the two men who were now halfway toward us.

I reached to pick up the ball we had thrown just

a moment before. My bare brown hand squeezed the seams as hard as I could, and I felt the rough black thread bite my fingers. The smooth white horsehair cover was unyielding, but I kept on squeezing it to keep from crying. When Jackie Robinson crossed over into the majors, I thought, he had Branch Rickey—general manager of the Brooklyn Dodgers—behind him to say, "Hey, he deserves to play." I didn't have a Mr. Rickey behind me. All I had was myself and seventeen years of loving the game.

I rotated the ball around and around in my palm until it felt strong and familiar again. And then I knew I had to throw it at least once. I wanted to throw that ball just as hard as I could at close range. Hard enough to smash that grin off that man's face. Hard enough to drive those two coaches right into the dust.

And so I drew myself in tight, cocked my front leg, reared back as far as I could go, and whipped my arm forward to throw. The black-and-white ball singed the air hard and fast across the open field. It landed right where I wanted it to—in the dirt just beyond home plate.

A yellow-haired player in uniform shaded her

eyes toward me, then bent down to pick it up. She stood there, they all stood there, whispering and looking right at me, no one daring to throw it back. The men saw it too. We were good, and we knew we were good. And now they knew it too.

"C'mon, Rita," I said, picking up my things. "It's a long way back to St. Cyprian's."

Bannecker Field

I don't know why they call it the sandlots. In my
time, I've played baseball in all kinds of places—
from manicured lawns with chalk lines sweet as
baby powder to smelly cow pastures where we had
to step gingerly and wait for the dirt clods to be
plowed smooth by lop-eared mules. Not once do I
remember playing in any sand. But when I was
scratching my way to where I could play baseball all
day, every day, it sure did feel like playing in a heap
of sand sometimes.

It was the spring of 1953. Two years after my
high school graduation and six after Jackie Robinson had first swung his way into the majors. Little
by little, more colored players had joined the ros-

ters of once all-white teams. But there still wasn't a spot for players in ponytails. Except in the sandlots.

Rita and I kept right on playing anyway—me, scooping up ice cream at a soda fountain during the week, and serving up strikes for St. Cyprian's on Sundays. Of all the recreational leagues in Washington, D.C., St. Cyprian's was the oldest and the best. If you ask me, I'd tell you that St. Cyprian's was even better than the Alexandria All-Stars, the semi-pro team in Virginia that Rita and I had played for the year before. I was all of sixteen when the All-Stars signed me.

Like St. Cyprian's, the All-Stars was an all-colored team, but the difference was—the All-Stars got paid. Imagine, getting paid for doing something you love! It wasn't much to speak of, pocket change, really. Most of it went for bus money for the ride across the river on game days. The way I figured it, I got to play baseball, so it was worth the trip. But after about a year of traveling back and forth, I decided to keep my ball playing in the city.

Sunday games at St. Cyprian's were just a stone's throw away. I could hop a streetcar from Mama's house and in twenty minutes I'd be toeing the rubber on Bannecker Field, where we played. The field was plunked down right in the middle of the city, with buildings on all sides. Across the street was Howard University, a college where coloreds could go and study to be doctors, lawyers, and preachers. Next to it was Myrtilla Minor's School for Colored Girls. When I stepped on the pitcher's mound, the U.S. Capitol was peeking over my left shoulder. Some evenings, you could hear the crowd noise from Griffith Stadium. That's where the all-white Washington Senators professional baseball team played. Where white fans could buy grandstand seats on the first-base line for a few cents apiece, and where Negroes could pay the same price to file into a sep-

View of Myrtilla Minor's School for Colored Girls with Bannecker Field in the foreground, 1949.
(From the Wymer Collection, The Historical Society of Washington, D.C.)

arate gate marked "Colored-Only" and sit in a separate seating area overlooking the left-field corner. Many a night I took to the mound with the scent of just-baked bread from the Wonder Bread bakery down the street. But as good as that white bread smelled, bringing to mind Grandma's Sunday morning kitchen, what I wanted a taste of more than any-

Corby Baking Company across the street from Bannecker Field, 1949. (From the Wymer Collection, The Historical Society of Washington, D.C.)

thing was just a chance to play in the big leagues. Until then, there was Bannecker Field.

No matter what sport you liked, Bannecker Field was a place you could go to practice being the best.

Bannecker Recreation Center, 1949. (From the Wymer Collection, The Historical Society of Washington, D.C.)

There were tennis courts, basketball hoops, a running track, even a swimming pool with a twelve-foot high dive. Jackie Robinson might have gotten permission to play with white boys, but there were only a few public places in the nation's capital where the rest of us coloreds could go to play sports. If you were a colored athlete at that time, Bannecker Field was the place to be. I guess that's what made it so easy for the man in the pinstripe suit to find me that one fine day.

"Look," Rita said to me as I was fixing to take the mound at the top of the ninth inning. "There he is again!"

"Hush up, Rita," I said. "You better keep your head in the game and stop looking all googly-eyed at some man in the stands."

"I ain't looking all googly-eyed," she said. "Besides, he's almost old enough to be my father. It's just that I been noticing him at every game for the past three weeks."

"Three weeks?" I said. "Well, if he's willing to sit on those hard stone steps they call bleachers to see us, I guess we'd better put on a show."

My arm was feeling especially good that day. I had held the other team to only one run, and we were ahead by one. There we were in the top of the ninth—only a few strikes away from a win—and my own team was making me work for it. It should have been a simple out. But a routine grounder had gotten by the first baseman, and now the other team had a runner on second with two outs. We'd hung on this far with a slim lead, but thanks to the error, the game was on the line. The other team was in scoring position. It was my job to shut them down cold.

The next batter up was a piece of cake. I had

pitched to this guy all day, and he never got further than sitting back down on the bench. It was the twitch of his eyebrows that let me know I had him nervous.

"No batter, no batter," yelled someone from the crowd, like he knew it too.

Now, pitchers gotta have two sets of eyes—one to watch the batter in front, and one to watch the base runner trying to steal. Somehow, without looking, I could feel that suit-wearing stranger watching me too. I knew I had an audience, so I was ready to strut my stuff.

Who-o-o-s-h! The first ball blew by the batter catching the outside corner of the plate. Strike one. He stepped out of the batter's box and pawed at the dirt with his cleats like he had dropped new money. I knew he'd be looking for the fastball again.

My next pitch was thrown inside, backing him off the plate. Ball one. Now, I wasn't trying to hurt nobody, but this was the fun part. Trying to get into the other guy's head and outthinking him each time. It's the only time that being a girl in baseball was a plus. Having a good arm was one thing. They could see that. But having a good head was another. Me being a girl, they just never saw it coming.

My third pitch was a breaking ball low and outside, but he brought his bat forward just enough to be called for strike two. Now I had the batter where I wanted him. He wouldn't know what to expect.

I looked to the catcher for his sign telling me what to pitch. He was calling for a fastball. I guess he thought, This guy can't hit it, so why trouble myself doing anything else. But I was showboating. That stranger in the stands was watching my every move. I could feel his eyes on me sure as I could feel that runner on second thinking about the steal. Not the runner, not the suit, I wasn't gonna let either of them get away without showing them what I could do.

I shook away the catcher's sign two times. The third time, he jumped up, took off his face mask, and called for time out. He ran out to the mound, his face balled up tighter than a fist.

"What do you think you're doing?" the catcher asked.

"I'm just having a little fun."

"Well, get the job done so we can get outta here," he said. "I don't wanna be too late getting home tonight."

"What's the matter, George?" I said. "Lucille fixing dumplings tonight?"

The catcher let go his face. "Hot rolls too! C'mon now."

But I had made up my mind what I was gonna do. And nobody's dumplings were gonna get in the way.

Who-o-o-s-h! Another breaking ball. They call it that 'cause just when you think it's coming right at you straight, it takes a little dip and gets clean out of the way of your bat. The batter swung and missed, and the umpire called, "Strike three." But George musta had his mind on them dumplings, 'cause instead of catching the ball square in his glove, the ball went sailing right on past him. The batter took off for first, and that runner on second base easily made it to third.

Now it was my turn to call time out and visit home plate.

"Just what in blazes is on your mind, George Wilson?"

He pushed his mask back off his face. "Sorry, Mamie," he said, grinning like a Cheshire cat. "Guess I messed up."

I was mad as a hornet, but it was impossible to really be mad at George. He played with a lot of heart, but to him it was only a game. He had a wife and two babies, and a good government job at the printing office. Baseball was just something to pass the time on a Sunday afternoon for George. It was different for me.

"Don't make me look bad out there," I said.

George put his face mask back on. "Don't worry about me, Mamie," he said, looking over his shoulder at the batter on deck. "He's the one you gotta worry about."

This next guy just happened to be one of the Savoy brothers—one of the best sandlot hitters in the league. All of the Savoys—boys and girls—lived and breathed sports. It was their religion. The Savoys had pretty much put this league together, and among them they had the dollars and talent to keep it going. This one was one of the older Savoys, and he knew and I knew that on any given day, a homer to him was like a walk in the park. In fact, he was the reason his team had scored at all. From the look of it, he was determined to snatch this game away from me.

With the tying run on third, a potential go-ahead

run on first, and a dangerous hitter at the plate, I was facing my greatest threat of the evening. I knew I couldn't pitch around him, and he knew that I knew it. I glanced over at the stands, and the man in the blue pinstripe was standing.

"Batter up," said the ump.

Savoy tapped his cleats with his bat, and his eyebrows didn't move at all. He was a big man who could intimidate any pitcher. His shoulders were like concrete and as wide as a city block. He set his jaw and wiggled his bat around as if to say: "Bring it on."

George flashed four fingers against the inside of his thigh to signal the pitch. But when he saw me shake it away, he leaned forward, balancing on his toes. He knew heat was coming.

Savoy let the first pitch go. It was a smart thing to do. If I threw a ball, no harm done. If I threw a strike, he'd be able to size up my speed and time his swing to get the most out of it. Strike one.

I bent over slightly at the waist, let both arms dangle free, and wriggled my shoulders to loosen up. Then I straightened up as far as my tiny frame would let me, and stared him straight in the chest. Not that I was afraid to look him in the eyes. I was concentrating on the strike zone, and he was a mighty big target. I stroked the seams on the horsehide for a while, set my pitch, then went into my windup. The pitch was low and right at his knees. The big man swung hard, but because I had held back my speed on the first pitch, he never expected the speed of the second. I knew my ninety-eight pounds couldn't outmuscle him, so I'd just have to let my little old brain outthink him. Strike two.

Rita yelped from second base, "Atta girl, Mamie. One more."

"Bring it on home," George yelled, pounding his catcher's mitt with his fist to show me the way.

Savoy stepped back off the plate and took a few hard cuts with his bat. Then, just before he stepped back into the box, he extended his arm straight out and pointed his bat right at me like some playground bully. I don't know if he was trying to make me mad or just scare the stripes right off my uniform, but I know it was exactly the wrong thing to do. 'Cause just at that moment, with the smell of fresh bread in my nostrils, the cheers from Griffith Stadium rising in my ears, the sun glinting off the Capitol dome in the distance, the man in pinstripes shading his eyes toward the mound, and a hunger in my belly that dumplings couldn't satisfy, I stretched myself up, whipped my arm forward, and sent a message right across the plate that Savoy couldn't deliver. He went down swinging on the hardest, fastest ball I probably had ever thrown. He had stranded the tying run, and the game was ours.

The next thing I remember was the gloves of my teammates patting me all around. And then the handshake of the man in the stands. He squeezed my right hand gentle, not because I was a lady, but like he knew it might be sore from pitching. His handshake was soft, but his hand was rough. It had the calluses of a man who'd been gripping a ball for years. Even though he was wearing a fine navy-blue pinstripe suit, starch-white shirt, and maroon tie, I realized this wasn't no doctor or preacher. This was a ballplayer.

"Pleased to meet you, Mamie," he said. "I'm Bish Tyson. Think you could be ready for a tryout a week from tomorrow?" He looked at me dead serious. I looked at Rita, who was just a-grinning.

"A tryout?" I said. "For what?"

"The Indianapolis Clowns are making a road swing through town next week. Ever heard of them?"

"Yes, sir," I said. "They're a colored team."

"A professional Negro Leagues baseball team," he corrected. "One of the best! They've asked me to keep an eye out for players like you."

For once, I couldn't think of a thing to say, even though Rita kept poking me with her glove from behind.

He continued, "They're looking for new talent—someone to make the crowd stand up and take notice. I think you just might be the ticket."

Well, the next thing you know, that Bish Tyson was telling me to bring my glove and my spikes to Bannecker Field that next Monday for a tryout.

Change-up

I could hardly sit through church that next Sunday, thinking about my Monday morning tryout. While the preacher was busy reciting the "Thou Shalt Not's," I was busy going over my list of "Gotta do's." Gotta get there in plenty of time to warm up. Gotta remember the liniment for my sore arm. Gotta bring an extra pair of shoelaces in case mine break while I'm lacing up. Gotta . . . Mama shot me a stern look more than once for toeing the pew in front of me like I was already on the mound.

Before the last note of the great Amen was sung at the end of service, I was off my seat and heading out the door to change for my 3:00 Sunday game at Bannecker. I'd been practicing my pitching hard all week to where my arm had gotten a little tender. But this would be the last time to get some game time in before the 10:00 tryout tomorrow. At the end of the game, my teammates, and even the players from the team we beat, wished me well. I knew that for them, coming to watch me play on a weekday morning would be difficult. I was really kind of glad, 'cause I was jittery enough on my own without having an audience to see me shake.

Sleeping that night was like trying to get butter from a duck. It was downright impossible. I kept turning things over in my mind: everything I had learned, everywhere I had been, and how everything I'd hoped for was resting on this day. I remembered my days at Grandma's house, where it all started, and my nights of talking to those big old stars. In Washington, D.C., streetlights hid the stars most nights. And tonight, on this important night, cloud cover kept even the few I was usually able to find hidden from sight. I strained to see just one from my bedroom window in Mama's house. Even the stars were telling me: "You're on your own this time."

When Mama came to wake me at 7:00 in the morning, my head was still resting on the windowsill where I had fallen asleep.

"Come on, baby," she said. "Get yourself washed up while I make you a good breakfast."

In no time, I was sitting at Mama's table staring into a plate of eggs, grits, and toast.

"Try and eat a little something, Mamie. You need your strength."

I stabbed at the yolk of my fried egg in silence.

"You know I want to be there with you today, honey," she said, grabbing me firm around both

Mamie (right) sitting on the front steps of her mother's house in Washington, D.C., with neighbor Carol Lee Thomas

shoulders. "But it's not easy changing shifts on short notice."

"I know, Mama." I smiled up at her. It was rare Mama ever missed a day's work as a dietician at Freedman's Hospital. I think it was because she liked helping people so much and she knew they depended on her. And raising a daughter on her own, she couldn't afford to lose a single day's pay.

"Why don't you stop messing with that plate, and go ahead and get out of here," she fussed.

"I'm sorry, Mama. I guess these butterflies flitting around my insides don't leave much room for grits."

"Child, I don't know what you're so nervous about," she said. "I've watched you grow up, both up close and at a distance. I've never known you to be afraid of anything." She turned me around by the shoulders and looked me straight in the eye.

"You go on out there and do like you always do, Mamie. You give it your best."

"I will, Mama," I said, my throat as dry as the cold toast on my plate.

"How many times have you told me that this is what you were born to do?" she continued. "Now, if that's true, all you gotta do is go out there and be yourself. And if they don't like what they see, then they're the losers, not you."

"Thanks, Mama," I said, squeezing both her hands hard like that day at Grandma's creek.

"You'll be just fine, honey," she said, turning to leave. "Besides, I prayed you up real good last night. You got exact change for the streetcar?"

"Yes, Mama, I got everything I need."

"You sure do, honey," she said, blowing me a kiss from the door.

Getting there at 9:30 for a 10:00 date, I thought I'd be early. But when I got to the field, I was surprised to see a bunch of folks already there. What I didn't see was anybody else that didn't know anyone but me. I was the only one trying out!

"Here she is, Mr. Haywood." I recognized Mr. Tyson, the man in pinstripes from last week. "That's the little lady I was telling you about."

"Pleased to meet you. It's Mamie, isn't it?"

"Yes sir, Mr. Haywood. Mamie Johnson."

"Bish was right. You're not much bigger than a minute. But he tells me you've got quite an arm."

"Thank you, sir," I said. "I might be little, but I can throw as hard as any man."

Mr. Haywood shook all over, laughing.

"Is that a fact? Well, that's something I'd like to see. Go on out there, Mamie, and show us what you got. All right, you all, let's warm her up."

The Indianapolis Clowns were swinging through town for a few days to play exhibition games before the regular season began. They'd played in Washington before, meeting teams like the Baltimore Black Barons and Washington Black Senators. They played in Griffith Stadium when the white professional baseball team was away. But this was the first time I was seeing them up close.

For the next hour, I played side by side with real ballplayers—Ted Richardson, Gordon "Hoppy" Hopkins, Junior Hamilton, and to my surprise, another lady baseball player, Lyle "Toni" Stone. They had me pitching to some of the best hitters in the league, asking me to try the pitches I knew and the ones I didn't. Then fielding. I was partial to shortstop, because it was closest to the mound, but they kept me rotating to see where I could fit in best. What surprised them as much as my pitching was my ability to hit. Sure, I did my share of swatting the breeze—I'd never been up against the likes of these fellas before. But I got my share of good cuts too—enough to let them know I could hold my own in the batter's box.

I can't remember exactly when I stopped being nervous, because I was having so much fun. When it was all over, Mr. Haywood seemed like he couldn't stop grinning. He shook my hand till it felt like it was gonna clean fall off, and then he took me to meet the team's business manager, McKinley Downs.

"Call me Bunny," he said, pumping my hand some more.

"Bunny," said Mr. Haywood, "you know what to do."

Seventeen years of waiting, and the only thing now between me and my dream was my name in ink on the bottom of the paper Bunny Downs was putting in my hands. I tell you, he didn't have to twist my arm one bit. This was the same Bunny Downs who just last year picked up some new cross-handed hitter from the sandlots down south. That slugger had been signed by the Milwaukee Braves after only two months. His name was Hank Aaron.

They say God made the world in one week. But I

don't think that was his biggest miracle. It had taken me all of my seventeen years to make it to this point. It only took the Good Lord seven days to take me all the way from the sandlots to a front seat on the Indianapolis Clowns' team bus. Me and my new teammates were heading down south to spring training.

Full Count

While most of the young ladies in Portsmouth, Virginia, were busy trying on Easter dresses and fancy bonnets, I was getting fitted for a brand-new uniform and ball cap. It was nothing like those flouncy little skirts the All-American Girls strutted around in. Their uniforms were cute and ladylike, but not too practical for sliding into base or kicking your leg up high to pitch.

Toni Stone and me—she was a fine second baseman signed by the Clowns the year before—we wore the exact same uniforms as the men on our team. And why not? We weren't there for window dressing. We were expected to play every bit as hard as the men, and we did. Our teammates mostly acted like gentlemen off the field, but as soon as we suited up, any kind of special treatment got left in the dugout.

I liked the color of the uniform—a field of royal blue with red stripes down the sides and red letter-ing to match. That tucked-in, belted-down, shin-length flannel uniform stuck to me like white on rice whenever I worked up a sweat. And there never was a game, or a practice, when I didn't. The town of Portsmouth, where the Indianapolis Clowns had spring training, was right on the waters of the Chesapeake Bay. The air was heavy and humid there, and you could taste the salt in it. So by the time I worked six or seven innings, I felt like a big wet dog in a heavy blue coat. But I wouldn't have traded in that uniform for nothing.

Now, any rookie showing up to camp the first week has got something to prove. And there I was a lady on top of it all. To make matters worse, it wasn't like I'd been signed to pick daisies somewhere in the outfield. I was gonna be right up in their faces, on top of the pitcher's mound. I knew all eyes would be on me the moment I stepped onto the field—my own teammates eyeing every pitch, catch-ing every mistake. But as nervous as that made me

Indianapolis Clowns pitcher Mamie "Peanut" Johnson, circa 1953

feel, it would have been twice as hard if Toni Stone hadn't made a way before me.

"I could tell some of the fellas didn't like my being there from the very first day," she said as we got ready for our first team scrimmage.

"Did they give you a hard time?" I asked.

"Most of them were nice enough to keep their opinions to themselves," she said. "But there was one rascal who wanted to let me know he didn't appreciate me one bit."

"What'd he do?"

"It was halfway through my first practice game. I was holding my own at second base. In fact, I had made quite a few good plays. Enough to let them know I wasn't just there for show."

"He called you an ugly name or something?"

"No, although there was plenty of snickering when coach put me in to cover second base—until my glove shut them up." She smiled and ringed her lips with red lipstick.

"Well, this fella had a chip on his shoulder bigger than a cinder block. I was on the bag at second, and he was the runner on first base. The whole time he was giving me the fish eye, like he couldn't wait to serve me up some trouble. Sure enough, the guy at

At age fifteen, Lyle "Toni" Stone quit her girls softball team and joined the Indianapolis Clowns. A second baseman and Mamie's teammate, Stone later signed with the Kansas City Monarchs. (Courtesy of the Negro Leagues Baseball Museum.)

the plate hit the ball sharp. The shortstop fielded the ball and lobbed it to me real soft. I looked up, and here comes bad news. That rascal was barreling into second, coming high and hard, right at me."

"Did he knock you down?"

"Worse," she said. "I've eaten my share of dust over the years, but I never had no one try to spike me like he did that day."

"Spike you?" I asked. "What do you mean?"

"He was coming at me like a freight train and went into a hard slide for second. I'd already snagged the ball, tagged second base, and was trying to make the play at first. But just as he slid into the base, he raised his top leg high and spiked me right in the shin."

"What happened after that?" I asked, retucking my socks and garters into my pants legs.

"Well, before I hit the ground good, Mr. Haywood came steamrolling off the bench right toward us. He was yelling that he had paid good money to sign me, and if anyone tried to put his drawing card at risk, he'd get a one-way bus ticket right home. I limped for days, but I didn't have much trouble after that."

I wondered if I'd get the same treatment. I'd been knocking birds off fences since I was five, and I'd played against guys all my life. These were supposed to be pros, but they were still just a bunch of guys. I caught myself in the mirror and saw Toni's reflection behind me. At that moment, I thought about Rita and the time the two of us had set out together to make the pros. Now here I was, in my brand-new uniform, stepping out for the first time as a professional ballplayer. And even though my stomach was jumping all around the way it had so many years ago, there was one big difference—I had already made the team. I straightened the bill of my cap and adjusted my ponytail out the back. I turned to face Toni.

"How do I look?"

"Like a winner!" she said, smiling. "I'm glad you're here, girl." Then she gave my ponytail a tug. "Now go out there and show them what you can do."

Life is full of first times you remember. Some are everyday things, like a first tooth falling out. Some are special, like a first kiss. Stepping out on the pitcher's mound my first time as an Indianapolis Clown was like the best "firsts" happening all at once. It was new crayons on the first day of school, the first sip of RC cola on a thirsty day, and the first peek under the tree on Christmas morning all rolled into one. I don't remember the score, who all was watching, or how many people were there. But I do remember that the first game I pitched was the first game I won. And just like all those other times when it really mattered, I knew, and my teammates knew, that I belonged.

The weeks that followed were filled with ordinary things. Now that I was on a pro team that played baseball just about every day, sometimes twice a day, I didn't pitch every game. When I wasn't

on the mound, Mr. Haywood used me as a utility in-
fielder, putting me wherever I was needed.

My days were filled with throwing and running
drills, practicing plays over and over until I could
turn them in my sleep. When I finally crawled into
bed each night, in the tiny little room at Old Lady
Purdie's rooming house where Toni and I stayed, I
was asleep before my head hit the pillow.

Once word got out that there was a lady pitcher
on the team, the crowds of locals coming to Com-
munity Field on Maltby Avenue to see us play
started swelling. Just like Mr. Downs had expected.
It wasn't much of a field to speak of, but there were
always plenty of folks who came out. There were
students from the Hampton Institute, a colored college nearby. Whole families who had been coming
to exhibition games since before the Clowns took
the Negro Leagues Eastern Division in 1949. White
folks too. We'd play anyone who scraped together a
team, like the white college team down the road or
the local rec club who always thought they could
beat us just because we were colored. In exhibition
games, we played farm teams like the Portsmouth
Merrimacs and the Lynchburg Cardinals. Even the
all-white, championship-winning Piedmont League

team—the Norfolk Tars. Because it was so crowded, colored ticket-holders sometimes had to wait at the Jim Crow entrance of Myers Stadium until nearly the fourth inning while the "Whites-Only" entrances stood empty. But the most exciting times were when other Negro League teams passing through, or retired legends of baseball on the barnstorming circuit, would give us a game. Giants like Leroy "Satchel" Paige.

Not all of my training in Portsmouth took place on the field. Off the field I had to learn which water fountains in town I was free to drink from. Which back doors of restaurants would serve me. What stores I was permitted to spend my money in. Just like I'd learned the rules of the game, in Portsmouth, I learned the rules for surviving in the South.

A lot of Southern towns still weren't ready to roll out the welcome mat for colored players, even the famous ones. So teams like ours had to be extra careful. Almost a decade after countless colored soldiers had spilled their blood on foreign soil during World War II, there were still plenty of battles for freedom to be fought right here at home. We knew that colored ballplayers, even those on major league teams, weren't allowed in any clubhouse in the South. They had to change in the bus. We knew that colored fans could pay to see the games, but had to leave the stadium to use the toilet. And even though Jackie Robinson had been playing in the majors for six years, newspapers like the *Afro American* reported that he was still getting angry letters threatening to kill him if he played in their towns. I guess there were still white people who didn't want their kids admiring Jackie Robinson, or any colored ballplayer, no matter how good they were.

As Southern towns go, Portsmouth, Virginia, was better than most. But it was one thing for whites to tolerate a colored player for a day or two while their favorite major league team was in town. It was another having a whole team of unknown colored ballplayers hanging around for months at a time during spring training. The Clowns had been training in Portsmouth for years, and so far there hadn't been too much trouble from the crowds of white folks who came to see us play. I guess you could say they got used to us. Still, I can't say I wanted to hang around there a minute more than we had to.

Finally, the day came when it was time to hit the

road for my first regular season with the Indianapolis Clowns. On the last night before we took off, Mr.
Haywood called us all together.

"Here's the schedule for the regular season," he
said matter-of-factly.

Then he rolled off the names of a dozen or more
cities we'd be visiting—Nashville, Memphis, Little
Rock, Atlanta, Birmingham, Louisville, Kansas
City, Chicago, Cincinnati, Baltimore, Philadelphia,
and Brooklyn, to name a few. Now, I had lived in
three places in my eighteen years, but I hadn't trav-
eled around much more than that. So the prospect
of visiting all those cities, even traveling on a
raggedy old bus in the summertime with no air-
conditioning, was exciting. But what Mr. Haywood
told us next was not.

"Now, I don't have to tell you that they're kicking
up trouble all over the South. There're boycotts in
Memphis, and bombings in Little Rock. And all because some folks don't believe colored folks deserve
the same rights as everybody else. In Birmingham,
Alabama, they still have a city ordinance against
whites and coloreds playing any kind of sports together. Down there, they'll fine you one hundred

dollars or six months in jail just for tossing the ball around.

"You regular players, you know the game plan. We go in. We play ball. We don't cause no trouble. You rookies"—he looked around at me and some of the other newcomers—"the idea is to keep your heads down and your mouths shut. We'll do our talking on the scorecards."

I couldn't sleep my last night in Miss Purdie's rooming house. I was excited to hit the road come morning, but wondered why some folks couldn't understand that playing ball wasn't supposed to hurt nobody. It was all about working together, playing well, and having fun. What difference did it make if you were white or colored, girl or guy, a city slicker or country as a mule? It was baseball just the same.

I tried to get in a few hours sleep before we headed out at 6:00 in the morning, looking to beat the heat. But my head was full of talk. Then I started worrying about some bad pitches I had made earlier that day. It had only been a practice game, but there still were a few pitches I wished I coulda taken back. Like the first ones I'd thrown to my teammate Gordon Hopkins in the third inning.

"Hoppy," as we called him, was one of the good guys. He played outfield and was a decent hitter. Well, I guess my mind musta been on something else, because before I knew it, I was behind three balls and two strikes. A full count. But if there's one thing I know about myself, it's that when the pressure's on, when my back's up against the wall, that's when I tend to do my best. It's like I can hear Bones and Uncle Ed speaking in my ear: "Just grit your teeth and fire it on in there." Well, on the next pitch, Hoppy was hopping back to his seat, struck out on a change-up to the inside corner.

Heading down the road to Dixie was something like a full count. I was full of promise and possibility, but at the same time, I knew I already had two strikes against me. I was colored, and I was a woman. But the game was just beginning, and the score hadn't been recorded yet. It was time to step up to the plate.

Call Me Peanut

We didn't win every game I pitched, but we sure won our share. Once I got over the opening-game jitters, I settled down into a nice, comfortable groove. If we had a doubleheader that day, Mr. Haywood would pull me after three or four innings and let one of the fellas pitch. That way I could rest my arm. But I pitched a little in every town because the team knew that having two women on the field meant extra tickets at the gate. That was important, because we got 60 percent of the gate if we won, 40 percent of the gate if we didn't. And with Mr. Downs paying each of us only around $200 twice a month, we needed as much of the gate as we could get. At the time, it was more money than I'd ever made in my life.

"What am I gonna do with all this cash?" I asked Hoppy my first payday.

"Keep a few dollars in your pocket, and set aside the rest for later," he said. "That money looks good now, but baseball's not a year-round game, you know."

It was true. Our schedule had us playing from April to October—150 games a season. The rest of the year we were on our own. For me, that meant spending the winter back in Washington with Mama, unless I came up with another plan. I knew I couldn't keep scooping up ice cream forever, and I knew that baseball, as much as I loved it, wasn't gonna last forever either. That's when I started thinking about going to college.

I'd always been a good student in school. It didn't matter to me whether it was the two-room schoolhouse in South Carolina, the all-white school I attended for about a year in New Jersey, or the colored-only classrooms of Long Branch once my aunt and uncle moved out of the projects. But I can't say I'd ever stopped to think about what to do with my life outside of baseball.

When I wrote Mama about the idea of going to college, she told me about cousins I had living in New York. Staying with them would cut down on expenses. It seemed simple enough to me—play ball in the spring, summer, and fall, and go to school during the winter term. Well the folks at New York University, where I applied, must have thought so too, because they sent me a letter saying, "Come on in." I studied medicine and engineering, 'cause next to baseball, I'd always liked fixing things. And I figured if boys could do it, I could do it too.

From that day on, I made it a habit of keeping a little piece of change for myself, and sending the rest back home to Mama. Some for her, and some for school. For the next two years, I hit the road during season play, and hit the books while my glove took a rest. Later on, there might be another career, even marriage and a family. But for now, there was baseball.

People always ask me if I minded playing on a team called the Indianapolis Clowns. It never takes me more than a minute to explain. Sure, we liked to cut up before the game. In fact, Mr. Downs even hired a comedian by the name of King Tut to travel with us. He had a gigantic baseball mitt, and we used to take turns throwing the ball to knock him

Comedian King Tut, outfielder Oscar Charleston, and Connie Morgan, 1954. Morgan played with the all-girls baseball team the North Philadelphia Honey Drippers, before signing with the Indianapolis Clowns. Charleston managed the Clowns in 1954. (Courtesy of the Negro Leagues Baseball Museum.)

down. But once the game ball was in play, it was no laughing matter. We took our baseball seriously, and clowning around was not what we were there to do.

Life on the road was no barrel of laughs either. It had its share of hardships. Bathrooms in the bushes, stale sandwiches on the bus. From town to town we'd sleep wherever we were allowed to. Most of the big cities we played in had decent enough hotels for colored guests. And the midsized towns usually had a rooming house or two to offer. But the pickings got slimmer the deeper south we went. Many a night we camped on church floors or slept all night on the bus. And we always welcomed the hospitality of colored families who'd take us in and fatten us up on corn bread, collard greens, and a sweet-potato pie or two.

Sometimes that raggedy old bus would break down and we'd wear our muscles out before the game pushing it uphill. And we never knew if we had enough gas to make it from place to place, 'cause some of the towns we stopped in had "Whites-Only" gas pumps. That never made sense to me. Seems like if those towns were so anxious to get rid of colored folks, they'd want to give us the gas we needed to get on down the road. But it wasn't all bad.

When we'd blow into town, the colored fans would treat us like movie stars. Win or lose, they always let us know how much they appreciated what we were doing. For them and for us, baseball was more than just a game. With every pitch we threw, with every play we turned, it was a chance to show the world that, underneath the skin, colored people were just like everybody else.

Blacks and whites back then lived in separate

worlds. They learned in separate schools, prayed in separate churches, drank from separate water fountains, lived on opposite sides of town. But when we played pick-up games with white teams along the way, we'd all be on the field together. And when those white families and those colored families came out to see us play, the boys and girls especially, you could almost feel a little bit of something crumbling down.

Another thing that seemed to change was how the fellas felt about girls being in the game. After getting used to the idea that me and Toni were there to stay, and that we could hold our own on the field, it was like we had twenty-six big brothers. They got real protective of us and made sure we were treated well. We paid them back by not beating them too bad when a card game broke out on the bus. We all helped one another keep our tempers in check whenever we faced a challenge on the field—from a bad day at the plate to a bad situation from the stands.

"Hey, girlie, that ain't no biscuit in your hand, is it?" yelled a rowdy spectator from the bleachers as I warmed up before a game in Birmingham. A ripple of laughter came down from the white fans. I pretended not to hear and just kept on throwing the ball.

"I said, you gonna serve some grits with that biscuit today?" he kept up.

"Don't mind him, Mamie, just keep looking right at me," said Oscar Charleston, a veteran outfielder who'd heard it all before.

"Whassa matter, girl? You deaf or something, or just plain disrespectful?"

Respect? I'd always heard that respect was treating folks the way you liked to be treated. And I didn't know nobody who liked to be treated like that.

I stopped throwing for a moment. "My name's Mamie, sir," I said right at him. "And I'm here to play some baseball."

Well, I won't repeat what he said next, 'cause I had my share of getting my mouth washed out with soap when I was a girl at Grandma's house. But it was a good thing that Oscar knew to grab me by the shoulders and, without saying a word, force me to the other side of the field right at that moment. Otherwise there woulda been a ruckus right then and there. Instead, he told me to take it out on every bat-

ter who faced me that day. He probably never saw
me throw so hard.

The fellas were always eager to help me learn
something new. Not just the ones on my own team,
but even the Negro Leagues players we played
against. We could be bitter rivals during the game,
but afterward, win or lose, we didn't pay it no mind.
The lesson I remember most was the one I learned
in Kansas City.

"That's a pretty fine arm you got," said the tall
lanky gentleman in the blue-and-white uniform.

"That's a pretty fine compliment, coming from
you," I answered politely.

Everybody knew Satchel Paige. The white newspapers had called him the "Chocolate Whizbang."
We called him a legend. He had played with a number
of Negro Leagues teams in his thirty-something-year
career: the Kansas City Monarchs, the Birmingham
Black Barons, the Pittsburgh Crawfords. He'd even
had his own team for a while in California—the
Satchel Paige All-Stars. Making more than $40,000
a year back then, he was the highest-paid player in
Negro baseball. More than forty years old, past re-
tirement age for most pitchers, Satchel Paige was

signed by the Cleveland Indians in 1948 as the first colored pitcher in the American League without ever setting foot in the minors. It was the same year that President Harry S Truman desegregated the armed forces. It was also the year the Cleveland Indians won the World Series. Retired now from the

Legendary pitcher Satchel Paige in 1943. He played with several Negro Leagues teams (including the New York Black Yankees) before being signed by the major league Cleveland Indians, and taught Mamie how to throw the curveball. (Courtesy of the Negro Leagues Baseball Museum.)

majors, here he was back in Kansas City playing with the Monarchs, the Negro Leagues team that had launched his greatness.

"Let me show you something that'll stop them in their tracks," he said, reaching for the ball.

Every pitcher has two or three favorite pitches they're good at. Me? I have a fastball and a change-up. And every now and then, I'd throw in Bones's old knuckleball just to keep the batter off guard.

Now Satchel, he had a reputation. He knew every pitch in the book. And when he got finished with the book, he wrote a few more pitches nobody had ever read before. He had a super fastball called a Long Tom and a slow fastball he called Little Tom. Then there was his humming Bee Ball. Any batter who ever hit one can still remember the sting. His Bat Dodger was a slider that lived up to its name. And his Hesitation Pitch drove batters crazy. It hiccuped its way to the plate. They finally outlawed it in the majors because, some say, it was striking too many people out. But whenever he played in Kansas City, he'd slip one in when they weren't looking. So when he wanted to show me something, you better believe I listened.

"The first thing you gotta do, little missy, is stop

squeezing the ball so tight." He cupped his long fingers around mine and relaxed my grip. "The next thing is, don't throw it directly over the plate. You want it to break to the outside."

He was poetry to watch. To see him move, so fluid and strong, was like watching a fast river running. He'd throw his leg way up in the air and bring his foot down with his body still moving. And when he guided my arm through the path of the pitch, I could feel the current of his delivery. He was one of the best pitchers anyone, colored or white, ever went up against. And here he was spending the time to teach me.

Well, he kept up like that for almost an hour before I finally got it down. And when I did, I felt like I knew how to make that ball mind my directions. Like getting a dog to mind, making it fetch or roll over. I was in control. Now, a curveball wasn't the kind of thing I would throw all the time, but I sure liked the idea of having something special to pull out of the bag whenever I got in trouble on the mound.

That's the very pitch I used two years later to shut down a power hitter on Satchel's very own team—Hank Baylis, a third baseman for the Kansas City Monarchs and one of the best hitters in the league.

Hank Baylis had a mean bat. To me, it was just like facing Savoy on Bannecker Field, only this wasn't the sandlots. And we weren't playing some no-'count team. This was the Negro World Series–winning, Satchel Paige–pitching, Kansas City Monarchs. And I was on the mound. Of all the games I played in my three years of professional baseball, this is the one I remember most.

"Be ready, baby. Just be ready," cried an old man sitting dead ahead of me in the stands. He had something to say with every pitch.

The game was tight, and I was only one out away from a cool drink of soda pop and a chicken dinner. I was past hungry, and my arm was tired. Baylis wasn't about to be embarrassed on his home field. He had to live in this town, and wasn't no woman gonna send him to the showers on a strikeout.

Just like Savoy, he took the first pitch. Strike one.

"What a pitch, baby. What a pitch," said the old man in the stands. Seems like he didn't care who won. He just wanted to see some good baseball.

Baylis was young, solid, and strong. And he had a good eye. So when I threw the second ball high and outside, he knew not to take it.

"Way to look," said gray hair. "That's a ball. You got her on the run now."

Baylis grinned at me, stepped back into the batter's box, and raised his elbows high. If I held up, this would be our last inning, and Baylis would be the last at-bat. The game would be ours, three to two.

Connie Morgan, a woman player who replaced Toni Stone, was in her stance near second base, ready for a force-out of the runner on first. Coach had waved the outfield way back, knowing Baylis could easily knock it out of the park. Third base was clean, and I wanted to keep it that way. Now, I could throw aspirins—pitches that would give hitters headaches—but this was hard work. And I didn't know if that ball was gonna do what I wanted it to do or go its own way like a misbehaving child.

I reared back, whipped my arm forward, and fired one in. Strike two.

I don't know who was more surprised—Baylis, me, or the man in the stands.

"O-o-o-o-o-o-o, Mama," said the noisy man above the cheers of the others in the half-filled stands. "Look out, Baylis. That little girl's gonna make you cry." The way he said it made everybody laugh. Even me. Concentrating as hard as I could, I couldn't hold back a smirk.

Baylis stepped out of the box and turned all the way around to face the stands. "Why, that little girl's no bigger than a peanut," he said. "I ain't afraid of her." The crowd roared.

I had to laugh too, 'cause he was right. Soaking wet and with my uniform on, I didn't weigh more than ninety-eight pounds. And when I drew myself up to full height, I wasn't no taller than five feet two inches, even with my spikes on. If it wasn't for my being on top of the mound, the folks in the stands wouldn't hardly see me at all. But there I was, a pitcher in full uniform on a professional team. And I had a job to do.

I was a peanut of a woman in a man's game. Even though we had several games left to finish the season, and scouts still buzzed around from time to time, I knew I would never see a day in the majors. Colored or white, Major League Baseball was off-limits to females. With three winning seasons to my credit, this was as far in baseball as I would ever be allowed to go. But little or not, my love for the game was as big and as powerful as any man's. So when I got ready to throw Baylis that pitch, I stood myself up as tall and proud as I could. I stretched my five feet two inches skyward and kicked my front leg high. I gripped the ball firmly, but not too tight, and I whipped my arm back, then snapped it forward like a slender black whip. Instead of throwing with my strong right arm, I threw that pitch with all my heart.

For a hitter, there are few things sweeter than the smack of the ball against the bat. But for a pitcher, there is no sound sweeter than the thud of the ball in the catcher's glove. Baylis liked to have broke his back swinging at that ball. But when all the noise stopped, Hank Baylis knew he'd been struck out by a little bit of nothing who just happened to have a curveball she'd been saving.

"Call me Peanut," I hollered to home plate. The crowd howled.

"That little Peanut sure took a bite out of you," cracked the man to Baylis and whoever else could hear.

The name stuck, and so does the memory of that day. But just like that curveball that rode the wind and turned in a different direction at the end, my life in baseball was getting ready to take a turn as well.

It was my third and last season with the Indianapolis Clowns. I had posted a 33 and 8 overall win record and a respectable batting average of .262 to .284. In between, there were visits back home to Mama and lots of talk about what would come next. Seems like no sooner had I got a foothold than I could feel the dream slipping away. The Clowns and the Negro Leagues as a whole were changing.

The majors had raided the Negro Leagues of so many top-notch players that making a living on the circuit became tougher than ever. Colored fans followed their favorite colored ballplayers in the majors. And colored teams like ours just couldn't compete. The curtain was closing on the era of the Negro Leagues.

It was the final innings of my days in professional baseball. But the one thing I learned in life is that, just like Satchel Paige's curveball, the Good Lord had a surprise pitch he was just waiting to serve me.

The letter I'd been waiting for came—I had been accepted into college once again, this time North Carolina A & T—and in just a few short years I would graduate and put on a new uniform and cap. The uniform of a registered nurse.

Miller's Field

"Negro Leagues Baseball Shop," says the young clerk. "May I help you? . . . Mamie 'Peanut' Johnson? Just a minute, please. Mamie," she says, "it's for you."

It's another reporter. He's asking me if I have any proof that I ever played the game.

"I've been covering baseball for thirty years," he's telling me, "and I never heard of you."

"Well, sir," I answer back, "I played pro baseball three years, and been in it more than sixty, and I never heard of you either. So I guess that makes us even." That's when I politely hang up the phone.

Every now and then I get some knucklehead coming in who refuses to believe I ever played the

Mamie works full-time in the Negro Leagues Baseball Shop in Capitol Heights, Maryland

game. But I can't say I blame them. There's no plaque on display commemorating Toni, Connie, or me in the National Baseball Hall of Fame, but you can see the skirted All-American Girls uniform hanging on display. And I hear they even inducted Canadian women in a hall of fame near Toronto. But every time a young person or an old-timer comes into the shop, I etch a little bit of history and a love for the game into their hearts.

"My daddy tells me you're thinking about putting together a little league," says a wide-eyed girl in pigtails asking me to autograph a baseball for her daddy's birthday.

"That's right, honey. Do you play?"

"I can hit pretty good, but Daddy says I could use a little help throwing. He says I throw like a girl."

"Boy or girl, the ball's not particular about who's doing the throwing," I tell her. "But let me show you how to throw like a winner. There's a field nearby, Miller's Field. Do you know it?"

"Can't say I do," says the girl's mother.

"It was where the Black farm team the Mitchell-ville Tigers used to play. And it was a practice field for the Washington Black Senators and Baltimore Black Elite. We're having an old-timers game there Sunday afternoon. Why don't you all come out? After I get off the mound, I'll be glad to show her a pitch or two."

More than Miller's Field had changed since I'd left the Clowns. Brick by brick, segregation was falling down. In 1954, the U.S. Supreme Court had finally agreed that colored children had the right to go to school with white children. But change like that didn't come easy. In 1955 colored folks' homes in Norfolk, Virginia, too close to white neighborhoods, were bombed. And colored players in Southern farm teams, drafted at last by the foot-dragging Washington Senators, were told to leave town by sundown or else risk getting hurt. A decade later, white fans, still unwilling to support integrated baseball in the nation's capital, caused the Washington Senators to move out of town. Griffith Stadium was torn down. In its place now is Howard University Hospital, staffed by the best Black doctors and nurses in the country. Shortly after I left the team, the Indianapolis Clowns withdrew from the league following a championship season. By 1961 the last of the Negro Leagues teams had folded.

I had changed too. For years, I had never looked further than playing professional baseball. By the age of twenty I had fulfilled that dream. So I started dreaming some new ones. Charles Johnson, who lived two blocks away from Mama all along, sweet-talked his way into marrying me. And from the first day I held him, our son, Charlie, became the love of my life. Mama still lives in our same house, and every now and then I see Rita in the neighborhood. Once in a while Hoppy drops by the shop or meets me on the field with his glove.

Do I have any regrets? Well, just a few. One is that Bones never got to see me play. After Grandma's house was sold away, he went further south to live.

Then just like me, he moved up north. There's not too much in the way of baseball in Connecticut where he lives now, at least no major league team. But I made sure that before I left the game, he had a piece of what he had started in me so long ago—one of my game balls, just like the one he had given me when I left for Long Branch.

I'm also sad that so many players, like home run–hitting Josh Gibson, never got the recognition they deserved. And that of the three women to play pro baseball—me, Connie Morgan, and Toni Stone—I'm the only one still living.

Mamie "Peanut" Johnson as she appears today, wearing her original Indianapolis Clowns uniform

Do I miss baseball? I can't say I do, 'cause working here at the Negro Leagues Baseball Shop, I'm surrounded by it every day. At sixty-six, my fastball has slowed down a bit, but when you see my name in the *Biographical Encyclopedia of the Negro Baseball Leagues,* it says: "The little right-hander could throw as hard as any male pitcher." Any fella who ever went up against me doesn't need a book to remember that.

I'm not finished with baseball, and from the look of things, baseball's not finished with me either. I

Mamie, in the summer of 2000, after throwing out the first ball at a Norfolk Tides minor league game at Harbor View Stadium, Virginia

got big dreams for Miller's Field. The weeds and
the run-down dugouts just don't know it yet. When
I close my eyes sometimes, I see it like it was. Full of
fly balls and good fielding. And families jumping up
and down in the stands. If I get my way, it will be like
that again one day.

After all, who would have thought there'd ever be
a wall in a Major League Baseball park with my name
on it? Its name is Miller too—Miller Park in Milwaukee, Wisconsin. And on that summer day in 2001
when they rededicated that wall, it was like it was
speaking to me and saying "I'm still standing and
so are you."

It took three years, hundreds of men, and tons of
equipment to build that new ballpark. Working
alone by word of mouth, it might take this old lady a
little bit longer to rebuild Miller's Field. Until then,
I'm keeping my arm limber. And there's still plenty
of baseball to hang my dreams on. It's all I've ever
needed to get along in life. Baseball, a dream, and a
strong right arm.

For More

Books

Adelson, Bruce. *Brushing Back Jim Crow: The Integration of Minor-League Baseball in the American South*. Charlottesville, Va.: University Press of Virginia, 1999.

Clark, Dick, and Larry Lester, eds. *The Negro Leagues Book*. Cleveland: The Society for American Baseball Research, 1994.

Dixon, Phil, with Patrick J. Hannigan. *The Negro Baseball Leagues, 1867–1955: A Photographic History*. Mattituck, N. Y.: Amereon House, 1992.

McKissack, Patricia C., and Fredrick McKissack, Jr. *Black Diamond: The Story of the Negro Baseball Leagues*. New York: Scholastic, 1994.

Organizations

The Historical Society of Washington, D.C.
Gail R. Redman, Library Director
1307 New Hampshire Avenue, N.W.
Washington, DC 20036-1507
(202) 785-2068
www.hswdc.org

National Baseball Hall of Fame and Museum
25 Main Street
P.O. Box 590
Cooperstown, NY 13326
Toll free: (888) 425-5633
www.baseballhalloffame.org

The Negro Leagues Baseball Museum
Raymond Doswell, Curator
1616 East 18th Street
Kansas City, MO 64108-1646
(816) 221-1920
www.nlbm.com

The Negro Leagues Outlet
Rivertowne Commons Shopping Center
6169 Oxon Hill Road
Oxon Hill, MD 20745
(301) 749-7200
www.negroleaguesoutlet.com/index.htm

Society for American Baseball Research (SABR)
812 Huron Road
Suite 719
Cleveland, OH 44115
(216) 575-0500
www.sabr.org

Yesterday's Negro League Baseball Players Foundation
P.O. Box 35674
Fayetteville, NC 28303
(910) 630-5190
www.ynlbpc.com

Miscellaneous Resources

All-American Girls
www.aagpbl.org

The Baseball Archive
www.baseball1.com

Black Baseball's Negro Baseball Leagues
www.blackbaseball.com

The They Played Baseball Foundation

In 1999, Mamie "Peanut" Johnson founded the They Played Baseball Foundation. Many ex–Negro Leagues ballplayers, including Mamie, yearned to pass down their baseball knowledge to younger generations but lacked the means to do so. The They Played Baseball Foundation provides this means.

The They Played Baseball Foundation:

♦ Is a non-profit organization dedicated to providing instruction to all children on the game of baseball

♦ Places an emphasis on good schoolwork and history, particularly of the Negro Leagues and other positive role models

♦ Teaches and instills life values through support, discipline, good sportsmanship, and respect for one's elders

✧ Will provide personal instruction and encouragement from professional baseball players and celebrities, past and present

✧ Will sponsor field trips for the children to baseball games, museums, and special events

✧ Is building an All-Star Team for regional competitions

For more information, contact:
The They Played Baseball Foundation
P.O. Box 1622
Mitchellville, MD 20717-1622
(301) 647-2145
www.theyplayedbaseball.com